PUMPKIN

PUMPKIN

50 cozy recipes for cooking with pumpkin, from savory to sweet

RYLAND PETERS & SMALL
LONDON • NEW YORK

Designer Paul Stradling
Editor Abi Waters
Head of Production Patricia Harrington
Creative Director Leslie Harrington
Editorial Director Julia Charles

Indexer Vanessa Bird

Published in 2024 by Ryland Peters & Small
20–21 Jockey's Fields
London WC1R 4BW
and
341 E 116th St
New York NY 10029

www.rylandpeters.com

Text © Nadia Arumugam, Ghillie Başan, Fiona
Beckett, Maxine Clark, Megan Davies, Ross Dobson,
Acland Geddes and Pedro da Silva, Brian Glover,
Dunja Gulin, Tori Haschka, Carol Hilker, Kathy
Kordalis, Tarek Malouf, Theo A. Michaels, Hannah
Miles, Isadora Popovic, Sarah Randall, Annie Rigg,
Laura Santini, Fiona Smith, Leah Vanderveldt,
Bea Vo, Fran Warde, Laura Washburn Hutton,
Lindy Wildsmith, Belinda Williams and Ryland
Peters & Small 2024.
Design and photographs © Ryland Peters & Small
2024.

ISBN: 978-1-78879-619-4

10 9 8 7 6 5 4 3 2 1

A CIP record for this book is available from the
British Library.
US Library of Congress Cataloging-in-Publication
data has been applied for.

Printed and bound in China.

NOTES

• Both American (Imperial ounces plus US cups)
and British (Metric) are included in these recipes
for your convenience; however, it is important
to work with one set of measurements only and
not alternate between the two within a recipe.

• All spoon measurements are level unless
otherwise specified.

• All eggs are large (US) or medium (UK), unless
specified as large, in which case US extra-large
should be used. Uncooked or partially cooked
eggs should not be served to the very old, frail,
young children, pregnant women or those with
compromised immune systems.

• Ovens should be preheated to the specified
temperatures. We recommend using an oven
thermometer. If using a fan-assisted oven,
adjust temperatures according to the
manufacturer's instructions.

• When a recipe calls for the grated zest of citrus
fruit, buy unwaxed fruit and wash well before
using. If you can only find treated fruit, scrub
well in warm soapy water before using.

CONTENTS

INTRODUCTION

Pumpkins belong to a vast family of gourds and squashes, all with their own merits and uses. They certainly shouldn't be relegated to only being used at Halloween or Thanksgiving, so be sure to seek them out whenever you can and add to your usual kitchen repertoire, using the wealth of recipes in this book for inspiration.

Pumpkins can take robust treatment when cooking. Roasting or pan-frying concentrates its flavor to a sweet, chestnutty richness. It makes a great base for soups and stews, but is also wonderful stirred into pasta or rice dishes. Its depth of flavor also works wonderfully when layered and baked in creamy gratins.

As you'll discover, it has a real affinity with a wide range of ingredients: its nutty sweetness works well with salty tastes such as goat cheese and it can be beautifully seasoned with musky sage, cumin or nutmeg, or the spicy heat of chile/chilli in a variety of dishes.

We mainly think of savory flavors when cooking with squash, but it picks up the sweetness of sugar too. Used in pies, tarts, and desserts, it cries out for warm spices such as cinnamon and ginger as well as a hint of citrus sharpness and the smooth richness of butter and cream.

If you find pumpkins difficult to get hold of, they are easily interchangeable with butternut squash or other winter squashes and can be prepared and cooked in the same way. Many of the recipes in this collection can be made using any kind of pumpkin or squash, so feel free to make use of whatever you have to hand.

From snacks and salads and soups and stews to pasta, pies, and other sweet treats, the recipes that follow are designed to help you discover the many savory and sweet delights of cooking with this wonderfully versatile ingredient. Enjoy!

ROASTING PUMPKIN

Many of the recipes in this book, call for pumpkin to be prepared and roasted before using. Follow these fail-safe instructions to achieve perfectly roasted pumpkin every time.

1 pumpkin or squash

2–3 tbsp olive oil

salt and black pepper

SERVES 4–6 (DEPENDING ON WHAT IT'S BEING USED FOR)

Preheat the oven to 350°F (180°C) Gas 4.

Peel and deseed the pumpkin or squash and chop the flesh into medium-sized chunks or wedges, depending on what you are using them for.

Tip the pumpkin onto a baking sheet and drizzle over the olive oil. Sprinkle over salt and pepper and use clean hands to thoroughly mix so that the pumpkin is well coated in oil.

Bake in the preheated oven for about 30 minutes, or until the pumpkin is tender and starting to turn golden around the edges.

Note: you can also add other flavorings, such as fresh or dried herbs, fresh or dried chile/chilli, and/or other spices when coating the pumpkin with oil, so feel free to experiment to find your favorite flavor combinations.

HOLLOWING OUT A PUMPKIN

If you need to hollow out a pumpkin or squash to use as a receptacle for a soup or stew, follow these instructions.

Use a pencil to draw a line around the top of the pumpkin, about 1½ inches/4 cm from the stalk. Take a knife and carefully cut off the top, following the pencil line, to make a lid for the pumpkin. You may need to gently lever the lid off if the seeds and fibers are attached to the lid.

Using a strong, small spoon, scoop out the seeds. When the seeds have all been removed, scrape the flesh out of the pumpkin so that the wall of the pumpkin is no more than about 1 inch/2.5 cm thick. Ensure that you do not make it too thin or you may pierce the skin.

Note: don't discard the pumpkin seeds. Wash them well in a bowl of cold water, then drain and transfer to a clean dish towel. Gently rub the seeds to clean off any fibers that may still be attached.

The seeds can then be roasted to make a delicious snack (often called pepitas), or used in other recipes, such as the moreish Pumpkin Seed Bars on page 102.

Try adding some flavoring to the seeds to change things up—a drizzle of maple syrup and a sprinkle of ground cinnamon work well, or try a sprinkle of chili/chilli powder, chili/chilli oil, and plenty of salt and black pepper to make a spicy snack.

GOURD-GEOUSLY GOOD FOR YOU

One-pots, soups & stews

PUMPKIN & MUSHROOM SOUP

3½ tbsp/50 g butter

2 white onions, diced

2 garlic cloves, finely chopped

1 small pumpkin, peeled, seeded, and diced

½ butternut squash, peeled, deseeded, and diced

6 cups/1.5 liters vegetable stock

2 cep mushrooms, finely sliced

¾ cup/200 ml heavy/double cream

salt and black pepper

TO GARNISH
chopped fresh parsley

fresh thyme leaves

truffle oil, for drizzling (optional)

SERVES 6

This deliciously rich soup is a wonderful, vibrant gold color. The silky nature of the cep mushrooms works really well with the smoothness of the soup and the addition of truffle oil, used at your discretion, elevates it from the everyday to something really special.

Melt three-quarters of the butter in a large saucepan and cook the onions, garlic, pumpkin, and squash until soft. Add the stock to the pan and bring to a boil. Reduce the heat and simmer for 15 minutes, until the pumpkin and squash are cooked.

Take the pan off the heat and blitz the mixture to a purée with a stick blender.

In a skillet/frying pan, heat the remaining butter and fry the ceps very gently for a few minutes, until softened but without coloring. Add the ceps to the soup and stir in the cream, then season to taste with salt and black pepper.

Ladle the soup into bowls and serve garnished with a sprinkle of fresh parsley and thyme leaves and a little drizzle of truffle oil, if you wish.

ROAST APPLE & PUMPKIN SOUP
WITH MAPLE NUT CRUMBLE

4 Pink Lady apples, peeled, cored, and roughly chopped into eighths

3 lb./1.4 kg pumpkin, peeled, seeded and chopped into pieces

2 onions, quartered

a 2-inch/5-cm piece of fresh ginger, peeled and sliced

6 garlic cloves, skin on

4 tbsp olive oil

6 cups/1.5 liters warm chicken or vegetable stock

2 tbsp each heavy/double cream and maple syrup

salt and black pepper

MAPLE NUT CRUMBLE

¾ cup/120 g mixed pumpkin seeds and nuts of choice

1 tsp salt

scant ½ cup/80 g superfine/caster sugar

SERVES 4

This warming and comforting soup is a surefire winner served with crusty bread for a satisfying lunch. It's delicious on its own, but to make it truly memorable for your guests, top with the nutty crumble.

Preheat the oven to 400°F (200°C) Gas 6.

Put the apple, pumpkin, onion, ginger, and garlic in a roasting pan. Drizzle with olive oil and season with salt and pepper. Roast for 45 minutes until golden. (Roast for another 30 minutes if you have time. This will give more color and sweetness.)

Remove from the oven. Squeeze the garlic from its skins and transfer the flesh to a saucepan. Add the pumpkin, apple, ginger, and onion and any juices from the roasting pan. Pour over the warm stock and stir to combine. Process with a stick blender until very smooth. Season with salt and pepper.

For the maple nut crumble, dry-toast the nuts and seeds in a skillet/frying pan. Pour them onto a baking sheet lined with baking parchment and sprinkle with salt.

Put the sugar in a pan and place over medium heat. Swirl the pan, rather than stirring, to mix the sugar as it melts. Cook until all the sugar has melted and has turned a light gold color. Pour the molten sugar over the top of the nuts. Be careful: the sugar will be very, very hot. Transfer the baking sheet to the freezer and chill for 30 minutes. Chop the praline on the baking parchment into rough pebbles.

Heat the soup through before serving, topped with the maple nut crumble, cream, and maple syrup.

ROASTED PUMPKIN SOUP

This warming soup freezes well so you can prepare ahead and then just defrost and reheat on the day.

3 lb./1.3 kg pumpkin or butternut squash, peeled, seeded and roughly chopped

grated zest and freshly squeezed juice of 1 orange

1 tsp ground ginger

3 tbsp olive oil

4 cups/1 liter chicken or vegetable stock

salt and black pepper

heavy/double cream, to serve

TOASTED TRUFFLE SEED MIX

3 tbsp pumpkin seeds

3 tbsp sunflower seeds

3 tbsp sesame seeds

1 tsp truffle salt

black pepper

SERVES 4

Preheat the oven to 350°F (180°C) Gas 4.

Place the pumpkin or squash in a roasting pan and sprinkle over the orange zest and juice, ginger, and olive oil. Roast in the preheated oven for 20–30 minutes until the squash is soft when you cut it with a knife.

Meanwhile, prepare the toasted truffle seed mix. Place all of the seeds in a dry skillet/frying pan together with the truffle salt and pepper. Stir with a spatula for a few minutes over the heat until the sunflower seeds turn a light golden brown. Take care that they do not burn, and tip out from the pan as soon as you've finished cooking.

Remove the roasted pumpkin or squash from the oven and place in a saucepan with the stock over a medium heat. Bring to a boil, then reduce the heat and simmer for about 15 minutes. Blitz in a food processor or blender until the soup is smooth (or use a stick blender).

Pour the soup into four bowls and add a swirl of cream to each. Serve topped with toasted seeds.

½ cup/70 g chopped leek (white part) or onion

4 tbsp olive oil

a pinch of sea salt

1⅔ cups/200 g pumpkin or squash, peeled, seeded, and cut into 1¼–1½-inch/3–4-cm pieces

1 cup/120 g carrot, cut into ¾–1¼-inch/2–3-cm pieces

1 tsp vegetable bouillon powder

¼ tsp ground turmeric

4 garlic cloves, crushed

2 bay leaves

3 dried tomato halves, chopped

2 tbsp cooking wine

¾ cup/150 g dried red lentils, washed and drained

2¾-inch/7-cm strip of kombu seaweed

4 cups/1 liter water

a squeeze of lemon juice

a little crushed black pepper

1 tbsp umeboshi vinegar

SERVES 4

PUMPKIN, CARROT & RED LENTIL SOUP

The addition of lentils makes this a more substantial and filling soup than most.

In a large saucepan, sauté the leek or onions in the olive oil with the salt, uncovered, until soft and transparent. Add the pumpkin or squash and carrot and sauté until the veggies start to "sweat." Add the bouillon powder, turmeric, garlic, bay leaves, and tomatoes and stir. Pour in the wine and let the mixture boil. Add the lentils, kombu, and water.

Turn up the heat, cover, and bring to a boil. Lower the heat and let simmer for 25–30 minutes or until the lentils and vegetables are completely tender.

At this point, remove the bay leaves. Use a stick blender to purée the soup and make it creamy, or leave as it is if you prefer it chunky.

Add the lemon juice, black pepper, and umeboshi vinegar and stir. Taste and add more spices if liked. You can add more hot water if the soup seems too thick, and it will definitely thicken as it cools.

2 tbsp sunflower oil

6¼ cups/750 g pumpkin or squash, peeled, seeded, and cut into chunks

a bunch of scallions/spring onions, chopped

a 2-inch/5-cm piece of fresh ginger, peeled and chopped

2 garlic cloves, chopped

2 lemongrass stalks, split lengthwise

2–3 fresh red chiles/chillies, deseeded and chopped, plus extra slices to garnish

a large bunch of cilantro/coriander, stalks and leaves separated

5 cups/1.2 liters vegetable or chicken stock

1 x 14-oz./400-ml can coconut milk

2–3 tbsp Thai fish sauce

freshly squeezed juice of 1–2 limes

crème fraîche or sour cream, to serve

salt

SERVES 6

SPICY PUMPKIN & COCONUT SOUP

This beautiful orange and green soup has a sweet-sour flavor and a spicy kick.

Heat the oil in a large saucepan over a low heat and cook the pumpkin and scallions with a pinch of salt for about 15–20 minutes until soft but not browned.

Meanwhile, put the ginger, garlic, lemongrass, chiles, and cilantro stalks in another pan with the stock and simmer, covered, for 20–25 minutes. Let cool slightly, then liquidize and strain into the pan with the pumpkin mixture. Discard the debris in the strainer/sieve, then liquidize again with the pumpkin mixture until smooth.

Return the soup to the rinsed-out saucepan, add the coconut milk, 2 tablespoons fish sauce, and the juice of 1 lime, then reheat, stirring, to just below boiling point. Add more fish sauce and lime juice to taste. Chop most of the cilantro leaves and stir into the soup (keep a few aside to garnish). Heat for a few minutes, but do not allow to boil.

Serve piping hot, topped with a spoonful of crème fraîche and scattered with the reserved cilantro.

ADZUKI BEAN & PUMPKIN STEW
WITH AMARANTH

Requiring little effort but with great rewards, this well-balanced, nourishing stew should be top of your list when you need some warming comfort food. The consistency is rich and creamy and the taste slightly sweet, satisfying your taste buds and leaving you feeling that little bit healthier.

1 cup/200 g dried adzuki beans

4 cups/1 liter cold water

1½ cups/180 g hokkaido or kabocha pumpkin, peeled, seeded, and cubed

⅓ cup/70 g amaranth

2 tbsp soy sauce

½ tbsp umeboshi vinegar

½ tsp ground turmeric

½ tsp sea salt

SERVES 2–3

Cover the adzuki beans with the water in a saucepan and soak overnight (this is not necessary but will speed up the cooking).

Bring the beans to a boil in the soaking water, then add the pumpkin and cook, half-covered, over a low heat for 30 minutes until the adzuki are half-done.

Add the amaranth and cook for 20–30 minutes until both the adzuki and amaranth are soft.

Season with the remaining ingredients and adjust the thickness by adding hot water, if necessary.

BEEF STEW WITH PUMPKIN & SZECHUAN PEPPER

4 tbsp dark soy sauce

1 tbsp crushed Szechuan peppercorns

1 lb. 5 oz./600 g sirloin steak, trimmed of fat and thinly sliced against the grain

3⅓ cups/400 g pumpkin or butternut squash, peeled, seeded, and diced

2 tbsp peanut oil

2 garlic cloves, thinly sliced

1 tbsp finely grated fresh ginger

3 tbsp sweet chili/chilli sauce

a small bunch of cilantro/coriander leaves, roughly chopped

½ fresh red chile/chilli, deseeded and thinly sliced, to garnish

SERVES 4–6

Fragrant Szechuan pepper gives a wonderful flavor and aroma to this dish.

Combine half the soy sauce and Szechuan peppercorns in a bowl, stir in the beef, cover, and marinate in the refrigerator for 20–30 minutes.

Bring a pan of salted water to a boil, then add the pumpkin or squash. Blanch for 5 minutes, or until tender. Drain well and set aside.

Heat the peanut oil in a wok or large skillet/frying pan until hot. Add the beef and stir-fry over high heat for 3–4 minutes, or until sealed. Remove the beef from the wok and set aside.

Add the garlic and ginger to the wok and stir-fry for 3–4 minutes until golden. Add the pumpkin with the sweet chili sauce, remaining soy sauce, and 1 tablespoon water. Bring to a boil, then reduce the heat and simmer gently for 2 minutes. Return the beef to the wok and stir-fry until cooked through.

Remove from the heat and stir in the chopped cilantro. Divide between 4–6 bowls and garnish with the sliced chile.

coconut or avocado oil, for frying

1 onion, finely diced

1 yellow (bell) pepper, deseeded and chopped into thin strips

1 tbsp grated fresh ginger

1 tbsp freshly chopped cilantro/coriander stems (leaves reserved for serving)

2 tbsp red Thai curry paste, or more to taste

1 cup/235 ml vegetable stock

2 cups/250 g pumpkin or butternut squash, peeled, seeded, and cut into chunks

1 x 14-oz./400-g can coconut milk

1 tbsp tamari

1 crown of broccoli, cut into small florets

1 cup/130 g frozen shelled edamame beans/green peas, thawed

salt

cooked rice or quinoa, to serve (optional)

SERVES 4

THAI PUMPKIN & VEGETABLE CURRY

This coconut curry is so packed with good vegetables that no-one will miss the meat.

Heat a thin layer of oil in a large saucepan over a medium-high heat. Add the onion, (bell) pepper, and a pinch of salt and cook for 5 minutes, stirring occasionally.

Add the ginger, cilantro stems, and curry paste and cook, stirring, for 1 minute. Add the vegetable stock and the pumpkin or butternut squash and stir to combine. Reduce the heat to medium, cover with a lid, and cook for 7–8 minutes.

Stir in the coconut milk, tamari, broccoli, and edamame beans or peas, cover with a lid, and bring to a boil. Reduce the heat and simmer for another 3–5 minutes until the pumpkin or squash and broccoli are tender and easily pierced with a fork. Remove from the heat and let stand for 5 minutes uncovered.

Taste for seasoning, adding more salt if needed, and serve warm over cooked rice or quinoa (if desired) and top with fresh cilantro leaves.

avocado or olive oil, for frying

1 onion, diced

3 cups/375 g pumpkin or butternut squash, peeled, seeded, and cut into ½-inch/1.5-cm cubes

2 tbsp tomato paste/purée

1 large garlic clove, finely chopped

3 tsp ground cumin

2 tsp smoked paprika

¼ tsp ground cinnamon

¼ tsp cayenne pepper

1 x 14-oz./400-g can crushed or chopped tomatoes in juices

2 x 14-oz/400-g cans black beans in their liquid

salt

TO SERVE (OPTIONAL)

diced avocado

sour cream

chopped large scallions/spring onions

corn chips

SERVES 4–6

PUMPKIN & BLACK BEAN CHILI

Cubes of pumpkin and black beans make this chili hearty and satisfying. The flavors deepen when it has time to sit, so it tastes even better the second or third time around.

In a large saucepan with a lid, heat enough oil to cover the base of the pan over a medium heat. Add the onion, season with salt, and cook for about 5 minutes until translucent. Add the pumpkin or squash and cook, stirring occasionally, for about 5 minutes.

Add the tomato paste, stir, and cook for 1 minute. Add the garlic, cumin, paprika, cinnamon, and cayenne pepper and cook for 1 minute more. Pour in the tomatoes and black beans along with the liquid from the cans. Season with salt and reduce the heat to medium-low. Cook, covered, for about 30 minutes, stirring occasionally, until the pumpkin or squash is tender. You may need to add ½ cup/ 120 ml or more water if the chili becomes too dry or thick for your liking.

Serve with your desired toppings.

TOO GOURD TO BE TRUE

Snacks, sharers & light bites

3 tbsp olive oil

¼ tsp hot red pepper/dried chilli flakes

3⅓ cups/400 g pumpkin or butternut squash, peeled, seeded, and diced

6 scallions/spring onions, thinly sliced

1 rounded tsp cumin seeds, lightly crushed

1 garlic clove, finely chopped

2 tbsp each finely chopped flat-leaf parsley and dill

7 oz./200 g feta cheese, diced

freshly squeezed lemon juice, to taste

8 sheets of phyllo/filo pastry, thawed if frozen

7 tbsp/100 g unsalted butter, melted

2 tbsp sesame seeds

salt and black pepper

MAKES 24 SMALL PASTRIES

SPICED PUMPKIN & FETA PASTRIES

The ideal party nibble to serve with drinks or a delicious treat for picnics.

Heat the oil in a large skillet/frying pan over a medium heat. Add the hot red pepper flakes and pumpkin and fry for 7–8 minutes until tender. Add the scallions, cumin, and garlic, then fry gently for another 2–3 minutes. Let cool, then mix in a bowl with the herbs and feta. Season to taste with lemon juice, salt, and pepper.

Preheat the oven to 375°F (190°C) Gas 5. Lightly grease one or two baking sheets. Working with one sheet of phyllo at a time (keeping the remainder covered to prevent drying out), cut each sheet lengthwise into three strips. Brush each strip with melted butter. Put a tablespoon of filling at one end of each strip, then fold up the pastry to enclose the filling in a triangle. Continue to fold up the strip of pastry to make a multi-layered triangle. Place on the prepared baking sheet and continue until all the phyllo and filling have been used. Brush each pastry with melted butter, sprinkle with sesame seeds, then bake for 20–25 minutes until crisp and golden.

ROASTED PUMPKIN GRILLED CHEESE SANDWICH WITH SAGE BUTTER

250 g/2 cups pumpkin or butternut squash pieces, fresh or frozen

4 slices white or sourdough bread

unsalted butter, softened

4 tbsp ricotta

2 thin slices mild cheese, such as Gouda or Fontina

1 tbsp vegetable oil

2–3 tbsp shredded/grated Parmesan

salt and black pepper

SAGE BUTTER

3 tbsp/50 g unsalted butter

a few sprigs of fresh sage, leaves stripped

a squeeze of fresh lemon juice

SERVES 2

This sandwich has a hidden twist thanks to the sage-infused butter.

Roast the pumpkin or squash following the instructions on page 8. Remove from the oven and crush coarsely. Set aside.

For the sage butter, melt the butter in a small saucepan until gently sizzling and beginning to deepen in color. Add the sage leaves and remove from the heat as soon as the leaves crisp up. Add the lemon juice and let stand until needed.

Spread softened butter on the outside of the bread on one side and spread two of the slices on the non-buttered side with the ricotta, evenly divided.

Put two slices of bread in a skillet/pan, butter-side down. If you can only fit one slice in the skillet, you'll need to cook one sandwich at a time. Top each of the bread slices with one slice of cheese and some of the crushed pumpkin, spreading evenly to the edges. Drizzle over liberal amounts of the sage butter, but no more than half per slice. Sprinkle half of the Parmesan over each slice and cover with the remaining bread slices, ricotta side down.

Turn the heat to medium and cook the first side for 3–5 minutes until deep golden, pressing gently with a spatula. Carefully turn with a spatula and cook on the second side for 2–3 minutes more or until deep golden brown all over.

Remove from the skillet, transfer to a plate, and cut in half diagonally. Let cool for a few minutes before serving. Repeat for the second sandwich if necessary. Any remaining sage butter can be drizzled over the sandwiches before serving.

5 oz./150 g thin slices prosciutto, cut into ¾-inch/2-cm strips

6¼ cups/750 g pumpkin, peeled, seeded, and cut into 1¼-inch/3-cm cubes

2 tbsp olive oil

2 tbsp fresh thyme leaves, plus sprigs to garnish

3 eggs

1 tbsp maple syrup

¼ tsp ground nutmeg

½ tsp sea salt

¼ tsp freshly ground black pepper

CELERY ROOT/CELERIAC SALAD

1 celery root/celeriac, shredded

3 tbsp chopped fresh flat-leaf parsley

2 tbsp good-quality mayonnaise

1 tbsp fresh lemon juice

1 tbsp olive oil

salt and black pepper

a 10-inch/25-cm narrow loaf pan, lightly oiled

SERVES 8–10

PROSCIUTTO & PUMPKIN TERRINE

This light, tasty terrine is fantastic for light lunches, and perfect to snack on.

Preheat the oven to 350°F (180°C) Gas 4. Lay the prosciutto across the width of the prepared loaf pan.

Toss the pumpkin with the olive oil and thyme leaves. Spread in a roasting dish and roast in the oven for 30 minutes until soft.

Leave the pumpkin to cool slightly, then put in a food processor and process to a purée. Add the eggs, maple syrup, nutmeg, salt, and pepper and process until well mixed. Pour the mixture into the loaf pan and bake for 30 minutes. Cover the terrine with a sheet of oiled foil and bake for 15 minutes until the pumpkin is set. Remove from the oven and leave to cool for at least 15 minutes before serving. Turn the terrine out, then invert so that the prosciutto is around the sides and base.

To make the celery root salad, toss all the ingredients together in a bowl.

Serve the terrine warm or at room temperature, garnished with thyme sprigs, with the salad.

1 small pumpkin (about 1½ lb/
670 g), peeled, seeded, and diced

2 tbsp olive oil

1 tsp black onion seeds

a pinch of spiced sea salt or
regular sea salt

4–5 curry leaves, crushed

1–2 garlic cloves, skins on

1½ cups/200 g self-rising/
self-raising flour, sifted

2 tsp baking powder

1 egg

1¼ cups/300 ml whole milk

3 tbsp melted butter, plus extra
for greasing

1 cup/125 g soft goat cheese

sour cream or crème fraîche,
to serve

a bunch of fresh basil leaves,
to garnish

pumpkin seed oil, to drizzle

salt and black pepper

ovenproof roasting pan, greased

SERVES 4

PUMPKIN & GOAT CHEESE PANCAKES

Perfect for a sophisticated lunch. Use a mild, creamy goat cheese so that the flavor is not too overpowering against the delicately spiced pumpkin.

Preheat the oven to 350°F (180°C) Gas 4.

Put the diced pumpkin in the prepared roasting pan. Drizzle with the oil and sprinkle over the onion seeds, salt, and curry leaves. Stir to coat the pumpkin in the oil and spices, then add the garlic cloves to the pan. Roast in the preheated oven for about 35–45 minutes until the pumpkin is soft and starts to caramelize at the edges. Let cool.

To make the pancake batter, put the flour, baking powder, egg, and milk in a large mixing bowl and whisk together. Season with salt and pepper. Add the melted butter and whisk again. The batter should have a smooth, dropping consistency. Add about two-thirds of the pumpkin to the batter and set aside.

Remove the skins from the garlic cloves and mash to a paste using a fork. Whisk into the batter, then crumble in the goat cheese. Mix together gently. Cover and put in the refrigerator to rest for 30 minutes.

Put a little butter in a large skillet/frying pan set over a medium heat. Allow the butter to melt and coat the base of the pan, then ladle spoonfuls of the rested batter into the pan, leaving a little space between each.

Cook until the underside of each pancake is golden brown and a few bubbles start to appear on the top— this will take about 2–3 minutes. Turn the pancakes over using a spatula and cook on the other side until golden brown. Remove the pancakes from the pan as they are ready and keep them warm while you cook the remaining batter in the same way.

Serve the pancakes topped with a spoonful of sour cream or crème fraîche, a few sprigs of basil, and the reserved pumpkin. Drizzle with pumpkin seed oil and sprinkle with black pepper.

PUMPKIN, BLUE CHEESE & SAGE PIZZA

Sweet-tasting pumpkin and tangy blue cheese are a winning combination in this delicious pizza that will delight your vegetarian friends and family.

1 ball of ready-made pizza dough

1 scant cup/100 g pumpkin or butternut squash, sliced and roasted (see page 8)

½ cup/60 g blue cheese, crumbled

⅓ cup/50 g mozzarella, torn

approx. 10 sage leaves (depending on size)

olive oil, to drizzle

salt and black pepper

pizza sheet or baking sheet dusted with semolina

pizza stone or large heavy baking sheet

MAKES 1 PIZZA

Put a pizza stone or a large, heavy baking sheet upside down on the top shelf of the oven.

Preheat the oven to 425°F (220°C) Gas 7 for at least 30 minutes.

Place the pizza dough onto the semolina-dusted pizza sheet and press outward from the center to flatten, making the edges slightly thicker than the center.

Scatter the dough base with the pumpkin, both cheeses, and sage leaves, then drizzle with olive oil and season. Transfer to the hot pizza stone or baking sheet and bake for 8–10 minutes until crisp. Serve hot with a little more olive oil drizzled over.

MINI CHEESE FONDUES

Serving fondue in baked pumpkin shells is not just about fun presentation—the sweet, tender squash is delicious to eat too!

4 small, mini pumpkins or round red onion (kuri) squash

3–4 tbsp olive oil

a few torn thyme sprigs

salt and black pepper

cubes of bread, to serve

FONDUE

2 tsp cornstarch/cornflour

1¼ cups/300 ml dry white wine

1 garlic clove, halved

1 bay leaf

14 oz./400 g Gruyère cheese, derinded and shredded/grated

2 tbsp Kirsch (optional)

9 oz./250 g Taleggio cheese, derinded and shredded/grated

4 tbsp sour cream

SERVES 4

Preheat the oven to 375°F (190°C) Gas 5.

Cut the lids off the squashes and take a thin slice off the bases so that they will stand without wobbling. Scoop out the seeds. Rub with the oil inside and out, season, and add a thyme sprig to each cavity. Bake in the oven for about 40 minutes. (Bake the lids as well, if liked, for around 20 minutes.) Save the flesh to use in another recipe.

Meanwhile, make the cheese fondue. Mix the cornstarch with 2–3 tablespoons of the wine and set aside. Put the remaining wine in a medium, heavy-based pan over medium heat and bring to a boil. Simmer for 2–3 minutes, then add the garlic and bay leaf and reduce the heat. Add the Gruyère and, stirring all the time, allow it to melt. When melted, remove and discard the garlic and bay leaf, then stir in the cornstarch slurry and the Kirsch (if using) until smooth. Add the Taleggio and stir over low heat until the cheese melts. Add the sour cream, season, and stir until you have a smooth texture.

Pour the fondue into the baked pumpkin shells, cover with the lids, if using, and serve with cubes of bread for dunking.

ROASTED FLAT MUSHROOMS
WITH SPICED PUMPKIN & CHICKPEA STUFFING

Warming and comforting, this is good enough to serve as a meat-free winter main (or use smaller mushrooms and serve as an appetizer).

1 small pumpkin (about 2 lb./900 g), peeled, seeded, and diced

5–6 tbsp olive oil

a small bunch of thyme

¼ tsp hot red pepper/ dried chilli flakes

1 garlic clove, chopped

1 x 14-oz./400-g can chickpeas, drained

½–1 tsp ground toasted cumin seeds

freshly squeezed lemon juice, to taste

1–2 tbsp chopped fresh flat-leaf parsley

1–2 tbsp crème fraîche (optional)

8 large, flat portobello mushrooms, stalks removed

4 tbsp toasted pumpkin seeds

salt and black pepper

SAUCE

1 garlic clove

a pinch of coarse sea salt

3–4 tbsp tahini

freshly squeezed lemon juice, to taste

4–5 tbsp plain/natural yogurt

SERVES 4

Roast the pumpkin mixed with the half the olive oil, most of the thyme, hot red pepper flakes, and garlic in a baking dish following the instructions on page 8. Let cool and put in a food processor with the chickpeas. Whizz to make a rough purée. Season to taste with salt, pepper, cumin seeds, and lemon juice, then stir in the parsley. If the purée is very dry, add the crème fraîche or a little water.

Meanwhile, put the mushrooms, gill-side uppermost, on an oiled baking sheet. Season and sprinkle with a few thyme leaves. Drizzle with the remaining olive oil and a good squeeze of lemon juice. Roast, uncovered, in the preheated

oven for 15 minutes until just cooked, then remove from the oven.

Distribute the stuffing between the mushrooms. Scatter with the pumpkin seeds and a few thyme sprigs. Spoon over a little of the mushroom cooking juices, then return them to the oven for about 10 minutes to heat through.

To make the sauce, mash the garlic with the salt in a bowl, then gradually work in 3 tablespoons tahini, followed by 1 tablespoon lemon juice. When smooth, gradually work in the yogurt, then taste and add more lemon juice and/or tahini as necessary. Serve alongside the roasted mushrooms.

PUMPKIN & GOAT CHEESE TARTS

Sharp goat cheese, caramelly sun-dried tomatoes and onion, and the scent of thyme all contrive to make this delicious savory tart.

1 pack of ready-made shortcrust pastry, chilled

3 tbsp olive oil

1 onion, thinly sliced

12 oz./350 g pumpkin, peeled, seeded, and diced

2 tsp chopped fresh thyme

5 oz./150 g goat cheese, crumbled

3½ oz./100 g sun-dried tomatoes in oil, roughly chopped

¾ cup/200 ml heavy/double cream

2 extra-large/UK large eggs

2 tbsp snipped chives

salt and black pepper

six 3½-inch/9-cm loose-bottomed metal tart pans

SERVES 6

Preheat the oven to 375°F (190°C) Gas 5. Roll out the chilled pastry thinly and line 6 individual tart pans. Protect the sides with strips of foil, then chill for a further 30 minutes. Transfer to a baking sheet and cook in the preheated oven for 12 minutes. Remove the foil and return them to the oven to cook for another 5–6 minutes until pale brown.

To make the filling, heat the oil in a skillet/frying pan and add the onion and a pinch of salt. Cover, reduce the heat to low, and cook, stirring once or twice, for 10–12 minutes until softened but not browned. Add the pumpkin and cook over medium heat, uncovered and stirring occasionally, until it is tender and lightly browned. Add the thyme, stir a few minutes more, then take off the heat and let cool.

Arrange the pumpkin, cheese, and tomatoes in the part-baked tart cases. Beat together the cream and eggs, add the chives, and season with salt and pepper. Carefully pour the mixture into the tart cases, return them to the hot oven and cook for about 25–30 minutes until the custard is set and puffed up. Let cool slightly before serving.

LIFE IS GOURD

Salads & sides

SPICED PUMPKIN & SPELT SALAD
WITH GOAT CHEESE

Spelt is rich in vitamins and minerals and works well in this tasty salad.

⅓ cup/50 g whole spelt

3⅓ cups/400 g pumpkin, peeled, seeded, and cut into large chunks

¼ cup/65 ml olive oil

½ tsp sea salt

½ tsp Spanish smoked sweet paprika

¼ tsp hot red pepper/dried chilli flakes

¼ tsp ground allspice

⅓ cup/50 g unsalted cashew nuts

1 tbsp white wine vinegar

4 oz./100 g soft goat cheese

4 handfuls of arugula/wild rocket

freshly ground black pepper

a baking sheet lined with baking parchment

SERVES 4

Put the spelt in a large saucepan with plenty of boiling water. Set over a high heat, bring back to a boil and cook for about 30 minutes until just tender yet still firm to the bite. Drain well and set aside.

Preheat the oven to 350°F (180°C) Gas 4.

Put the pumpkin in a bowl with half of the oil, salt, paprika, hot red pepper flakes, and allspice and toss to coat. Tumble the pumpkin onto the prepared baking sheet and pour over any spiced oil from the bowl. Bake for about 20 minutes. Remove from the oven, scatter over the cashews, and return to the oven for 8–10 minutes, until the cashews are golden and the pumpkin tender.

Combine the remaining oil and vinegar in a bowl.

Put the spelt, pumpkin, cashews, goat cheese, and arugula in a large bowl and gently toss to combine, being careful not to break up the cheese or pumpkin too much. Pour over the dressing and season well with black pepper. Serve immediately.

PEARL BARLEY & PUMPKIN SALAD

Pearl barley is a great addition to salads as it manages to retain a bit of texture and works beautifully with roasted pumpkin.

4 cups/500 g pumpkin, peeled, seeded, and cut into 1¼-inch/ 3-cm cubes

olive oil, for roasting and drizzling

generous 1 cup/200 g pearl barley

14 oz./400 g green beans, topped but not tailed

3½ oz./100 g sun-dried tomatoes, roughly chopped

20 pitted/stoned black olives

1 tbsp capers

1 red onion, sliced

a bunch of fresh basil, roughly chopped

1 garlic clove, crushed

salt and black pepper

SERVES 4–6

Preheat the oven to 400°F (200°C) Gas 6. Toss the pumpkin with a little olive oil and sea salt in a roasting pan. Roast for 20–25 minutes until soft but not disintegrating.

Meanwhile, bring a pan of salted water to a boil and cook the pearl barley for 20–30 minutes. You want the grains to be al dente, but not chalky or overly chewy. Once ready, drain and set aside.

For the beans, bring another pan of salted water to a boil and prepare a bowl of ice water. Add the beans to the pan and cook for 3–5 minutes. Test them by giving them a bend; you want them to be flexible, but still have a nice snap if you push them too far. Once cooked, drain them and drop them immediately into the iced water. This "refreshing" process will halt the cooking process and help keep the beans perfectly cooked and vibrantly green.

To assemble the salad, mix the pearl barley with the sun-dried tomatoes, olives, capers, red onion, basil, and garlic. Add this to the roast pumpkin and green beans and stir gently until well combined. Drizzle with a little olive oil and serve.

ROASTED PUMPKIN, CHICKEN & LENTIL SALAD WITH PRESERVED LEMON DRESSING

This combination of pumpkin, sharp lemon, and earthy lentils is so good. It's best made with a freshly roasted chicken, but it can be made in advance for a party. You'll need to roast a whole chicken for this, stuffing it with a halved lemon and some garlic cloves and basting with a little olive oil and lemon.

2 cups/400 g Puy lentils

2 bay leaves

2–3 shallots, peeled

1 pumpkin or butternut squash, peeled, seeded, and cut into 1–2-inch/2.5–4-cm chunks or slices

6 oz./180 g cherry tomatoes

8–9 tbsp extra virgin olive oil

1 large fennel bulb, trimmed and cut into ½-inch/1-cm pieces, feathery tops reserved and chopped

1–2 tsp wholegrain Dijon mustard

½ tsp runny honey

tarragon white wine vinegar or freshly squeezed lemon juice, to taste

4 tbsp chopped fresh flat-leaf parsley

2–3 tbsp chopped preserved lemon (rind only)

1 small freshly roasted chicken (about 3½–4½ lb./1.75–2 kg), carved and torn into shreds, skin discarded

a handful of arugula/rocket or baby spinach leaves, to serve

salt and black pepper

SERVES 6–8

Preheat the oven to 375°F (190°C) Gas 5. Rinse the lentils and put them in a saucepan with the bay leaves and one of the shallots, halved. Cover with cold water, bring to a boil, and then simmer gently for 30–40 minutes until cooked.

Meanwhile, toss the pumpkin and tomatoes with 2 tablespoons of the oil on a baking sheet. Season with salt and pepper and roast, uncovered, stirring once, for 25 minutes, or until tender and browned. The tomatoes should be collapsed but still juicy.

Heat 1½–2 tablespoons of the remaining oil in a skillet/frying pan. Add the fennel with a pinch of salt and fry it gently for about 5–6 minutes until softened but still with a bite.

Chop the remaining shallot(s) finely. In a bowl, whisk the remaining oil, mustard, and honey together and add tarragon vinegar or lemon juice to taste (about 2–3 teaspoons). Season well with salt and pepper.

When the lentils are cooked, drain and toss, while still warm, with the dressing. Toss in the roasted pumpkin, tomatoes, fennel, parsley, reserved fennel tops, preserved lemon, and chicken. Adjust the seasoning to taste and toss in the arugula just before turning onto a serving platter.

ROASTED PUMPKIN WITH SPICED LENTILS, GOAT CHEESE & WALNUTS

This recipe will fill your kitchen with appetizing and exotic aromas. You can use butternut squash or sweet potato in place of the pumpkin, or a combination of the two, as long as the weight is roughly the same.

1⅓ cups/275 g green lentils, rinsed and drained

¼ cup/50 g walnut pieces

1 small pumpkin, peeled, seeded, and cubed

3 tbsp olive oil

1 large onion, halved and sliced

1 fresh red chile/chilli, halved, seeded, and sliced

1 tsp ground cumin

1 tsp ground turmeric

1 tsp paprika

2 garlic cloves, crushed

14-oz./400-g can chopped tomatoes

a pinch of sugar

a large handful of fresh flat-leaf parsley leaves, chopped

a small handful of fresh cilantro/coriander leaves, finely chopped

freshly squeezed juice of ½ a lemon

8 oz./250 g soft goat cheese or feta

salt and black pepper

crusty bread, to serve

SERVES 4

Preheat the oven to 375°F (190°C) Gas 5.

Put the lentils in a saucepan with sufficient cold water to cover. Add a pinch of salt, bring to a boil, and simmer for 20–30 minutes until tender. Drain and set aside.

Dry roast the walnuts in a small skillet/frying pan set over a low heat until browned. Set aside.

Arrange the pumpkin cubes on a baking sheet, toss with 2 tablespoons of the oil, and sprinkle with a little salt. Roast in the preheated oven for about 30–35 minutes until tender, turning halfway through cooking time.

Heat the remaining oil in a large saucepan, add the onion, and cook over a low heat for 3–5 minutes until soft. Add the chile, cumin, turmeric, paprika, garlic, and a pinch of salt and cook, stirring, for 1 minute. Add the tomatoes, sugar, another pinch of salt, half the parsley, and half the cilantro. Simmer, uncovered, for 20 minutes, stirring in the cooked lentils about 5 minutes before the end of cooking

time, just to warm through. Taste and adjust the seasoning if necessary.

Add the roasted pumpkin, the remaining herbs, and a squeeze of lemon juice. Taste and adjust the seasoning.

Crumble over the goat cheese, add the walnuts, and serve immediately with plenty of crusty bread.

ROASTED PUMPKIN WEDGES
WITH LIME ZEST & SPICES

1 medium-sized pumpkin, halved lengthwise, seeded, and cut into 6–8 segments

2 tsp coriander seeds

1 tsp cumin seeds

1 tsp fennel seeds

1–2 tsp ground cinnamon

2 dried red chiles/chillies, chopped

2 garlic cloves

2 tbsp olive oil

coarse sea salt

finely grated zest of 1 lime

6 wooden or metal skewers, for serving (optional)

SERVES 6

This is a great way to enjoy pumpkin. Serve these spicy wedges on their own or with any grilled, roasted, or barbecued meat or poultry dish. Save the seeds and roast them lightly with a little oil and coarse salt as a nibble.

Preheat the oven to 400°F (200°C) Gas 6.

Using a mortar and pestle, grind all the dried spices with the salt.

Add the garlic and a little of the olive oil to form a paste. Rub the mixture over the pumpkin wedges and place them, skin-side down, in a baking dish. Roast them in the preheated oven for about 35–40 minutes, or until tender.

Sprinkle over the lime zest and serve hot, threaded onto skewers, if using.

STUFFED SUGAR PUMPKINS
WITH PESTO & GOAT CHEESE

Choose small sugar pumpkins or butternut squash for this recipe (or just use the bottom half and keep the top piece for other recipes).

4 small sugar pumpkins or butternut squash, washed and dried

2 small red onions, diced

16–20 cherry tomatoes, halved

a large handful of basil leaves

4–8 tbsp pesto

2 small goat cheeses or mozzarella, torn into pieces

olive oil, for drizzling

salt and black pepper

SERVES 4

Preheat the oven to 400°F (200°C) Gas 6. Cut off a "lid" from the pumpkins and reserve. Scoop out the flesh with an ice-cream scoop to make a smooth container.

Put the onions in a strainer/sieve set over a bowl and cover with boiling water. Leave for 2 minutes, then drain, pat dry with paper towels, and distribute among the pumpkins. Add the tomato halves, the basil leaves, a generous tablespoon or two of pesto, then the goat cheeses or mozzarella. Sprinkle with salt and pepper. Each of the hollows should be nicely filled with the ingredients.

Brush the pumpkins all over with olive oil, brushing the top of the cheese. Set the "lids" slightly askew. Arrange in an oiled roasting pan or dish and bake until tender. Test with a metal skewer after about 20 minutes, then every 5–10 minutes until done (the time will depend on the size of your pumpkins).

Note: if using small butternuts, halve lengthwise and scoop out the seeds. If large, cut them off just as they start to narrow into a waist—you're aiming for a hollow receptacle.

ROAST PUMPKIN WITH SWEET POTATO MASH & MARSHMALLOWS

Try this as a Thanksgiving side dish—a whole roast pumpkin, filled with sweet potato mash, and topped with marshmallows!

1 medium pumpkin

vegetable oil, for roasting

4 large sweet potatoes, diced

2 whole cloves

1 cinnamon stick

3½ tbsp/50 g butter

⅓ cup/75 ml heavy/double cream

1 tsp white granulated sugar

1 tsp ground cinnamon

¼ tsp ground nutmeg

¼ tsp ground ginger

1 tsp runny honey, plus extra to drizzle

¼ cup/30 g halved pecans

¼ cup/30 g mini marshmallows

salt

SERVES 4

Preheat the oven to 425°F (220°C) Gas 7.

Cut the top off the pumpkin and discard. Using a spoon, scoop out the seeds and discard. Drizzle a little oil into the pumpkin, season, and roast for about 40 minutes, or until it is lightly browned at the edges and the inside is cooked through. Once cooked, remove from the oven and set aside.

Meanwhile, put the sweet potatoes in a pan and cover with tepid water. Add the cloves, cinnamon stick, and a pinch of salt. Bring to a boil and cook, uncovered, for 30 minutes, or until a knife passes through them with little resistance. Drain the potatoes, remove the cinnamon stick and cloves, and return to the pan. Add the butter, cream, sugar, ground cinnamon, nutmeg, and ginger and mash well. Add the honey and season with salt to taste.

Spoon the sweet potato mash into the pumpkin. Top with the pecans, mini marshmallows, and a drizzle of honey. Serve warm as a side dish.

ROAST PUMPKIN & GARLIC POLENTA

Pumpkin and garlic are cleverly used here for a lighter polenta that is still full of flavor, without lavish amounts of butter and cheese.

1 medium pumpkin or 1 large butternut squash

5 large garlic cloves, unpeeled

3 tbsp sunflower or grapeseed oil

3 tbsp/40 g butter

1¾ oz./50 g Parmesan cheese, shredded/grated, plus extra to taste

generous 2 cups/250 g good-quality Italian polenta/cornmeal

5 cups/1.2 liters vegetable stock, plus a little extra as necessary

salt and black pepper

a large roasting pan

SERVES 6

Preheat the oven to 375°F (190°C) Gas 5.

Halve the pumpkin. Cut one half into quarters and scoop out the seeds. Quarter the other half, scoop out the seeds, cut each quarter into 2 or 3 pieces, and cut away the skin with a sharp knife. Put all the pumpkin in a roasting pan along with the garlic cloves. Drizzle with the oil, mix well together, and season generously with salt and pepper. Roast in the preheated oven for about 35–40 minutes until soft.

Remove the pumpkin from the pan and set the small pieces aside. Scrape the flesh off the unpeeled quarters and place in a food processor. Pop the roasted garlic cloves out of their skins and add to the pumpkin and whizz until smooth. Add the butter and Parmesan, whizz again, and season.

Cook the polenta in the stock, following the packet instructions, whisking well to avoid lumps. Add the pumpkin purée and mix well. Add a little extra stock if needed to give a slightly sloppy consistency. Add more salt, pepper, and Parmesan to taste. Reheat the pumpkin pieces briefly in a microwave or skillet/frying pan and serve on top of the polenta.

PUMPKIN, CORN & BREAD PUDDING
WITH CHEESE & CHIVES

1 tbsp olive oil

1 onion, halved and thinly sliced

1½ cups/375 ml whole milk

1 cup/225 ml light/single cream

3 eggs, beaten

a small bunch of chives, snipped

leaves from a small bunch of fresh parsley, finely chopped

1 baguette, cut into ¼-inch/5-mm slices

2 cups/300 g corn/sweetcorn kernels, canned or frozen

about 1 lb./450 g pumpkin or butternut squash, peeled, seeded, and sliced

1 cup/100 g sharp/mature Cheddar, grated

salt and black pepper

a 12 x 8-inch/30 x 20-cm baking dish, very well buttered

SERVES 4–6

Any kind of cheese can be used here, so it's a good way to use up odds and ends.

Preheat the oven to 375°F (190°C) Gas 5.

Heat the oil in a large skillet/frying pan. Add the onion and cook over a low heat for 3–5 minutes until soft. Season lightly and set aside.

Combine the milk, cream, and eggs in a bowl and whisk to combine. Season with 1½ teaspoons salt. Add the chives and parsley, mix well, and set aside.

Arrange half the baguette slices in the prepared baking dish in a single layer; you may need to tear some to cover all the space. Put half the onion slices on top, then scatter over half of the corn kernels. Arrange half of the pumpkin slices evenly on top and sprinkle with half of the cheese. Repeat one more time (bread, onion, corn, pumpkin, cheese). Stir the milk mixture and pour it evenly all over the pudding. Cover tightly with foil and bake in the preheated oven for 20 minutes.

Remove the foil and continue baking for about 30–40 minutes, until golden. Serve immediately.

PUMPKIN & TOMATO CHUTNEY

1 lb./450 g firm pumpkin or butternut squash, peeled, seeded, and cut into ½-inch/1-cm cubes

1 cup/200 g ripe tomatoes, skinned, seeded, and chopped

1 cup/200 g onions, chopped

⅔ cup/25 g golden raisins/sultanas

1¼ cups/250 g soft brown/demerara sugar

1 tsp salt

1-inch/3-cm piece of fresh ginger, peeled and finely chopped

1 garlic clove, finely chopped

a little freshly grated nutmeg

1 cup/200 ml malt vinegar, plus ½ cup/100 ml extra

1 clean, dry, warm jar, 1 pint/500 ml, with lid or cover

waxed paper disc

MAKES 1 PINT/500 G

There are many varieties of pumpkin and this recipe can be used to preserve all of them. Make sure that the flesh is firm and not stringy, or it will spoil the finished texture of the chutney.

Put the pumpkin, tomatoes, onions, golden raisins, sugar, salt, ginger, garlic, nutmeg, and the 1 cup/200 ml vinegar in a saucepan and bring slowly to a boil. Simmer for 1 hour, stirring from time to time. The chutney should look dark, dense, and rich. Top up with extra vinegar if the chutney dries out too much while cooking.

Transfer to the jar, cover the surface of the chutney with a waxed disc, wipe the jar with a clean, damp cloth, and seal at once. Label when cool and store for 1–6 months in a cool, dark place before opening.

GO BIG OR GOURD HOME!

Pasta & rice dishes

PUMPKIN & SAGE MAC 'N' CHEESE

1 lb./450 g macaroni

a handful of coarse sea salt

1 pumpkin (2 lb./1 kg), peeled, seeded, and cubed

3 tbsp vegetable oil

2 tbsp/30 g butter

2 shallots, finely chopped

2¾ cups/650 ml heavy/double cream

leaves from a few sprigs of fresh sage, finely chopped, plus whole leaves to garnish

1¼ cups/100 g shredded/grated Grana Padano or Parmesan

¾ cup/100 g shredded/grated Cheddar

1 cup/50 g fresh breadcrumbs

salt and black pepper

SERVES 6–8

Earthy sage and sweet pumpkin are a match made in heaven.

Cook the macaroni in a saucepan of salted boiling water according to the packet instructions.

Preheat the oven to 400°F (200°C) Gas 6. Roast the pumpkin following the instructions on page 8, then set aside.

Heat the butter and the remaining oil in a saucepan. Add the shallots and cook over a high heat for 2–3 minutes, stirring, until golden. Add the cream, sage, and a pinch of salt and bring to a boil, then reduce the heat. Add the cheeses and stir well to melt.

Preheat the broiler/grill to medium–hot.

Put the cooked macaroni in a bowl with the pumpkin. Pour over the cream sauce and mix. Taste and adjust the seasoning.

Transfer the macaroni mixture to a baking dish and spread evenly. Top with a good grinding of black pepper and sprinkle the breadcrumbs over the top. Broil/grill for 5–10 minutes until the top is crunchy and golden brown. Serve immediately garnished with sage leaves.

TAGLIATELLE WITH PAN-FRIED PUMPKIN & RED PEPPER OIL

The pumpkin makes this a wonderfully warming pasta dish for a cold winter's evening.

1 tbsp light olive oil

3⅓ cups/400 g pumpkin or winter squash, peeled, seeded, and chopped into 1-inch/2.5-cm pieces

14 oz./400 g pappardelle, tagliatelle, or any other ribbon pasta

finely grated zest and juice of 1 unwaxed lemon

1¾ oz./50 g arugula/rocket leaves

a large handful of chopped fresh flat-leaf parsley

salt and black pepper

RED PEPPER OIL

1 small red (bell) pepper, sliced

6 large red chiles/chillies, sliced

1 small red onion, sliced

4 garlic cloves, peeled but left whole

1 tsp cumin seeds

¼ cup/65 ml olive oil

SERVES 4

Preheat the oven to 350°F (180°C) Gas 4.

Put the red (bell) pepper, chiles, onion, garlic, cumin seeds, and 2 tablespoons of the olive oil in a roasting pan. Cook in the preheated oven for 1 hour, turning often. Transfer the contents of the roasting pan to a food processor while still hot. Add the remaining oil and whizz until smooth. Let cool, then pour the mixture into a clean and dry screwtop jar.

Heat the light olive oil in a skillet/frying pan set over a high heat and add the pumpkin. Cook for 10 minutes, turning often, until each piece is golden brown all over.

Meanwhile, cook the pasta according to the packet instructions and drain well.

Put it in a large bowl and add 2–3 tablespoons of the red pepper oil. Add the cooked pumpkin, lemon zest and juice, arugula, and parsley and toss to combine.

Season well with salt and pepper and serve immediately.

Note: the remaining oil will keep for 1 week when stored in an airtight jar in the refrigerator. It can be added to tomato-based sauces and soups for extra flavor.

PUMPKIN & CHICORY PASTA BAKE

This pasta bake is a wholesome veggie dish that really hits the spot. You could try it with other roasted veg, but sweet root veg works best.

1¾–2 lb./800–900 g pumpkin or butternut squash, unpeeled and chopped into 1-inch/2.5-cm chunks

3½ tbsp/50 g butter

6 tbsp/50 g all-purpose/plain flour

2¾ cups/650 ml whole milk

½ cup/40 g shredded/grated Parmesan, plus extra to top

2 heads chicory, leaves separated and cut in half lengthwise

8–10 dried lasagne sheets

1¼ cups/250 g ricotta cheese

1 oz./20 g fresh basil

salt and black pepper

SERVES 6

Preheat the oven to 425°F (220°C) Gas 7. Roast the pumpkin or squash following the instructions on page 8 until tender and lightly caramelized.

Melt the butter in a saucepan set over a medium heat and once sizzling, add the flour. Mix very well and cook for a couple minutes. Add a splash of milk and allow the milk to be absorbed before you add another splash. Continue this process until all the milk is used. Let the sauce cook and thicken for about 5 minutes, stirring constantly—it should end up with a custard-like thickness. Remove from the heat, add the Parmesan, stir to combine, then season well (make sure you taste it).

Scatter a layer of pumpkin on the base of a baking dish, followed by chicory, some dollops of ricotta, then a layer of lasagne sheets. Top with the white sauce and a scattering of basil. Repeat the layers, continuing until you've used up all the ingredients. Finish with a scattering of basil and a sprinkle of Parmesan. Bake for 40 minutes until tender, golden brown on top, and bubbling.

PUMPKIN & SAGE PASTA

This cozy pasta dish is like fall/autumn on a plate and is quick and easy to make, so is perfect for a weeknight supper.

½ pumpkin or butternut squash, peeled, seeded and chopped into ½-inch/1-cm cubes

16 sage leaves

olive oil, for drizzling

½ tsp hot red pepper/dried chilli flakes

7 oz./200 g dried pasta or 6 oz./ 160 g fresh pasta (e.g. orecchiette)

4 tbsp/60 g butter

freshly squeezed juice of ½ lemon

2 tbsp pumpkin seeds, toasted

⅓ cup/70 g smooth goat cheese, crumbled

salt and black pepper

2 heaped tbsp finely grated Parmesan, to serve

SERVES 2

Preheat the oven to 350°F (180°C) Gas 4.

Roast the pumpkin with eight of the sage leaves and the hot red pepper flakes following the instructions on page 8 until the pumpkin is softened and the sage leaves are crisp.

Cook the pasta in a large saucepan of salted water following the instructions on the packet.

Meanwhile, heat the butter, lemon juice, and remaining sage leaves in a heavy-bottomed pan. When the butter begins to color, but not burn, remove the pan from heat. Add the roasted pumpkin (but not the crispy sage leaves), combine, check the seasoning, and set aside.

Drain the pasta, but keep a cup of the cooking water. Tip the pasta into the pumpkin and butter, add the pumpkin seeds and a splash of the retained cooking water, and toss with gusto over a high heat until the pasta looks creamy and well coated. Serve immediately topped with the crumbled goat cheese, crispy sage leaves, and plenty of Parmesan and extra freshly ground black pepper.

PAN-FRIED PUMPKIN & WALNUT PASTA
WITH PARSLEY & WALNUT SAUCE

Traditionally, a version of this walnut sauce is served with pappardelle pasta in northern Italy, but it is good with other shapes too.

5¼ oz./150 g fresh walnut halves

2–3 fat garlic cloves, peeled

5 tbsp olive oil

1 tbsp walnut oil

5 tbsp crème fraîche or sour cream

a small bunch of flat-leaf parsley

freshly squeezed lemon juice, to taste

5½ cups/650 g pumpkin or squash, peeled, seeded, and cut into ½-inch/1-cm slices or chunks

1–2 pinches of hot red pepper/dried chilli flakes, crushed

14 oz./400 g pasta of your choice

freshly grated nutmeg, to taste

salt and black pepper

freshly grated Parmesan, to serve

SERVES 4

Preheat the oven to 350°F (180°C) Gas 4.

Put the walnuts on a baking sheet and toast them in the preheated oven for 5–6 minutes, making sure they don't burn. Turn them onto a dry, clean dish towel/tea towel and rub vigorously to remove as much of the skin as possible. Chop a third of the nuts roughly and set aside, then put the remaining nuts in a food processor.

Blanch the garlic in boiling water for 2–3 minutes, drain, and rinse. Put the garlic in the processor with the walnuts, add 2 tablespoons olive oil, the walnut oil, and cream. Whizz to make a paste. Set aside a third of the parsley, then whizz the remaining two-thirds into the sauce. Chop the reserved parsley and set aside. Leave the sauce in the processor until needed.

In a large skillet/frying pan, heat the remaining olive oil over a medium heat, add the pumpkin or squash and hot red pepper flakes and cook, turning the pumpkin now and then, for about 10–12 minutes until it is tender and lightly browned.

Meanwhile, bring a large saucepan of salted water to the boil and cook the pasta according to the packet instructions.

When the pasta is cooked, drain, reserving 4–5 tablespoons of the cooking water. Whizz enough of this water into the sauce to make it creamy, then season with salt, pepper, and a little nutmeg. Toss the pasta with the pumpkin or squash, remaining walnuts and parsley, and a little of the sauce. Serve the Parmesan and remaining sauce at the table.

PUMPKIN & GORGONZOLA RISOTTO

By roasting the pumpkin first, before adding it to the risotto, it retains its deep flavor and unique texture. The salty Gorgonzola, stirred in just before serving, perfectly complements the sweet-tasting pumpkin.

4 cups/500 g pumpkin, peeled, seeded, and cubed

1 tbsp light olive oil

4 cups/1 liter vegetable stock

2 tbsp/30 g butter

1 leek, halved lengthwise and thinly sliced

1 garlic clove, chopped

1½ cups/300 g risotto rice

1¾ oz./50 g Gorgonzola cheese, crumbled

SERVES 4

Preheat the oven to 350°F (180°C) Gas 4. Roast the pumpkin following the instructions on page 8.

Put the stock in a saucepan and heat until gently simmering. Melt the butter in a saucepan over a high heat and add the leek and garlic. Cook for 4–5 minutes, stirring often, until the leeks have softened but not browned.

Add the rice to the leeks and stir for 1 minute, until the rice is well coated with oil. Add ½ cup/125 ml of the hot stock to the rice and cook, stirring constantly, until the rice has absorbed most of the liquid. Repeat this process until all the stock has been used—this will take about 20–25 minutes. The rice should be soft but still have a slight bite to the center.

Add the roasted pumpkin pieces. Remove the pan from the heat, stir in the Gorgonzola, and serve immediately.

PUMPKIN & PEA RISOTTO WITH TOASTED PUMPKIN SEEDS

1 stick/125 g unsalted butter

3 tbsp pumpkin seeds

¼–½ tsp ground chili/chilli

about 4 cups/1 liter vegetable or chicken stock

1 large onion, finely chopped

4 cups/500 g fresh pumpkin or butternut squash, peeled, seeded, and finely diced

1½ cups/300 g risotto rice

3 tbsp chopped fresh mint

1½ cups/200 g frozen peas, cooked and drained

¾ cup/75 g shredded/grated Parmesan cheese

salt and black pepper

SERVES 6

A vivid orange color speckled with green peas, this risotto is a delight to eat.

Melt half the butter in a saucepan until foaming, then add the pumpkin seeds. Stir over a medium heat until the seeds begin to brown, then stir in the chili, salt, and pepper. Remove from the heat.

Put the stock in a pan and keep at a gentle simmer.

Melt the remaining butter in a saucepan, add the onion, and cook for 10 minutes until soft. Add the pumpkin or squash and cook, stirring, for about 15 minutes until it begins to soften. Mash the pumpkin in the pan, then stir in the rice. Cook for a couple of minutes to toast the grains.

Begin adding the stock, a ladleful at a time, stirring until the stock has almost been absorbed by the rice. Don't let the rice dry out—add more stock as needed. Continue for about 15–20 minutes until the rice is tender and creamy, but the grains still firm.

Taste and season well with salt and pepper and stir in the mint, peas, and all the Parmesan. Cover and let rest for a couple of minutes, then serve sprinkled with the pumpkin seeds.

PUMPKIN & RICE GRATIN

Unlike a conventional gratin, this version has rice, which gives it a more interesting texture and makes it more substantial.

12½ cups/1.5 kg pumpkin, peeled, seeded, and cut into small cubes

3 tbsp olive oil

½ cup/100 g long grain rice

a sprig of fresh thyme

3 tbsp fresh breadcrumbs

a small handful of fresh flat-leaf parsley, finely chopped

3 tbsp crème fraîche or sour cream

2½ oz./75 g Gruyère cheese, finely shredded/grated

salt and black pepper

a large baking dish, greased with butter

SERVES 6

Put the cubed pumpkin in a large saucepan with about 2 tablespoons of the oil, a pinch of salt, and 1 cup/ 250 ml water. Cook over a low heat for about 20–30 minutes, stirring, until soft and adding more water as needed.

Meanwhile, put the rice and the remaining oil in a separate saucepan and cook over a medium heat, stirring to coat the grains. Add 1 cup/250 ml water, the thyme, and a pinch of salt and bring to a boil. Cover and simmer for 10 minutes, until almost tender. Drain and discard the thyme.

Preheat the oven to 400°F (200°C) Gas 6. Mix the breadcrumbs with the parsley and a pinch of salt. Set aside.

Mash the pumpkin into a coarse purée with a wooden spoon and stir in the cooked rice and crème fraîche or sour cream. Taste—the topping and cheese will add flavor, but the pumpkin mixture should be seasoned as well. Spoon the mixture into the baking dish. Sprinkle the cheese over the top, then the breadcrumbs. Bake for about 20–30 minutes until browned. Serve hot.

PUMPKIN GNOCCHI WITH BUTTERY SAGE BREADCRUMBS

These gnocchi are light and yet deeply satisfying. They can be prepared in advance and frozen and stored for up to six months.

a starchy, dry-fleshed pumpkin or squash (about 1 lb. 10 oz./750 g), halved and seeded

1 lb./450 g medium floury potatoes, unpeeled, washed, and pricked

1⅓ cups/180 g all-purpose/plain flour, sifted with ½ tsp baking powder, plus extra flour as needed

⅓ cup/50 g fine semolina, plus extra for dusting

½ cup/100 g Parmesan cheese, freshly shredded/grated, plus extra to serve

freshly grated nutmeg, to taste

7 tbsp/100 g unsalted butter

1 garlic clove, peeled and halved

¼ cup/30 g white breadcrumbs from day-old bread

10 sage leaves, shredded

salt and black pepper

SERVES 4

Preheat the oven to 400°F (200°C) Gas 6.

Line a baking sheet with lightly oiled foil. Put the pumpkin, cut-side down, and the potatoes on the sheet. Bake in the preheated oven for 1 hour, until soft. (Check the pumpkin after about 40 minutes—if cooked, remove it and continue baking the potatoes.)

When cool enough to handle, scrape the pumpkin flesh off the skin and do the same with the potatoes. Using a mouli-légume or strainer/sieve, purée the vegetables into a bowl. Do not use a food processor as it will make the potatoes too gluey. While the puréed vegetables are still warm, work in the flour and semolina using a fork. Add more flour as necessary to make a malleable mixture. Work in half of the Parmesan and season well with salt, pepper, and nutmeg.

Dust a work surface with semolina. Take about one-third of the mixture and roll it out to form a long, thin sausage shape about ¾ inch/2 cm thick. Cut into 1-inch/2.5-cm lengths. Roll each piece along the tines of a fork, then in a little semolina and set on a dish towel-covered tray, dusted with more semolina. Repeat with the remaining mixture.

Bring a large saucepan of salted water to a boil. Meanwhile, heat half the butter in a skillet/frying pan over a medium heat with the garlic. Let the garlic sizzle for a few minutes, then add the breadcrumbs and half the sage. Fry gently until the breadcrumbs turn crisp and golden brown. Discard the garlic.

In a separate pan, melt the remaining butter, add the remaining sage and keep warm. When the water boils, turn it down to a simmer and cook the gnocchi in batches until they bob to the surface, then cook for 1–2 minutes more. Use a slotted spoon to transfer them to a warmed serving dish.

Toss with the butter and sage, then with the breadcrumbs. Serve immediately, offering extra Parmesan.

THE REASON FOR PUMPKIN SEASON

Breads, cookies & cozy bakes

PUMPKIN RAISIN BREAD

This sweet golden bread tastes beautiful plain or buttered, or spread with strawberry conserve and cream.

2¾ cups/400 g strong white bread flour

½ tsp salt

1 sachet easy-blend dried yeast

4½ tbsp/65 g unsalted butter

1½ cups/190 g cooked mashed pumpkin

½ cup/125 ml heavy/double cream, warmed

½ cup/75 g raisins

1 egg, beaten, to glaze

a 2-lb./1-kg loaf pan, greased

MAKES 1 LARGE LOAF

Sift the flour and salt into a large bowl, stir in the dried yeast, and rub in the butter. Add the mashed pumpkin, cream, raisins, and ¼ cup/65 ml lukewarm water. Mix to form a soft but not sticky dough, adding more flour or water as needed. Turn out the dough onto a floured surface and knead for about 10 minutes until smooth and elastic. Return to the bowl and cover. Let rise at room temperature until doubled in size—about 1–1½ hours.

Knock down the risen dough. Turn out onto a well floured surface and knead briefly. Shape into a loaf and press neatly into the prepared pan. Cover and let rise as before until doubled in size—about 45 minutes.

Preheat the oven to 400°F (200°C) Gas 6 .

Brush the risen loaf with beaten egg, then bake in the preheated oven for 25 minutes. Reduce the temperature to 350°F (180°C) Gas 4 and bake for a further 15–20 minutes or until the turned-out loaf sounds hollow when tapped underneath. Cool on a wire rack before slicing and serving.

PUMPKIN LOAVES

3 small pumpkins, tops cut off and discarded

olive oil, for drizzling

¾ cup/100 g gluten-free self-rising/self-raising flour plus 2 tsp baking powder (OR ¾ cup/100 g gluten-free all-purpose/plain flour plus 3 tsp baking powder and ½ tsp xanthan gum)

⅔ cup/100 g fine cornmeal/polenta, plus extra for sprinkling

2 eggs

4 tbsp/60 g butter, melted and cooled

1¼ cups/300 ml whole milk

1 tsp hot smoked paprika

1 tbsp pumpkin seeds

pumpkin seed or olive oil, for drizzling

salt and black pepper

MAKES 3 SMALL LOAVES

This gluten-free bread is made with pumpkin purée so is a vivd orange color.

Preheat the oven to 350°F (180°C) Gas 4.

Place the pumpkins in a roasting pan and drizzle with olive oil. Put them in the preheated oven and roast for about 30–40 minutes until the flesh is soft but the pumpkins still hold their shape. Remove from the oven and leave to cool.

When the pumpkins are cool, use a spoon to scoop the flesh and pumpkin seeds from the insides to hollow out the shells. Discard the seeds.

Preheat the oven again to 350°F (180°C) Gas 4.

Sift the flour and baking powder (plus xanthan gum, if using) into a mixing bowl and add the cornmeal and 2 tablespoons of the cooked pumpkin (save the rest for another recipe). Add the eggs, butter, milk, and paprika and whisk until smooth. Season with salt and pepper, then divide the mixture between the pumpkins and return to the roasting pan. Sprinkle with pumpkin seeds and drizzle with a little pumpkin seed or olive oil. Bake for 25–35 minutes until the bread is cooked through. The loaves are best eaten on the day they are made.

PUMPKIN SCONES

Pumpkin purée, flavored with maple syrup, cinnamon, and vanilla, makes these gluten-free scones so moist and absolutely delicious.

2½ cups/300 g pumpkin or butternut squash, peeled, seeded, and chopped into 1¼-inch/3-cm pieces

3 tbsp/40 ml pure maple syrup

2 tbsp vanilla extract

1 tsp ground cinnamon

2⅔ cups/350 g gluten-free self-rising/raising flour plus 1 tsp baking powder (OR 2½ cups plus 1 tbsp/340 g gluten-free all-purpose/plain baking flour plus 3 tsp baking powder and 1 tsp xanthan gum)

1 cup/100 g ground almonds

1 stick/115 g butter

¼ cup/50 g superfine/caster sugar

a baking sheet, greased and lined
a 3-inch/7.5-cm fluted cutter

MAKES 14

Preheat the oven to 375°F (190°C) Gas 5.

Put the pumpkin pieces on a large piece of double layer of foil. Drizzle over the maple syrup and vanilla extract and sprinkle with the cinnamon. Wrap the foil up well and transfer to a baking sheet. Bake for 30–40 minutes until the pumpkin is soft. Let cool, then purée in a food processor.

Put the flour, baking powder, and ground almonds in a mixing bowl and rub in the butter with your fingertips. Add half the pumpkin purée and sugar to the flour and mix in. Gradually add the remaining purée a little at a time, until you have a soft dough. You may not need all the purée, depending on the water content of your pumpkin.

On a floured work surface, use a rolling pin to roll out the scone dough to ¾-1¼ inches/2–3 cm thick. Stamp out 14 rounds using the cutter. Arrange the scones on the prepared baking sheet a small distance apart.

Bake in the preheated oven for 12–15 minutes until the scones are golden brown and sound hollow when you tap them. Serve warm or cold. These scones are best eaten on the day they are made.

PUMPKIN MADELEINES WITH SAGE

These sweet, dainty madeleine cakes make a tasty accompaniment to soups and stews but can be eaten on their own as a snack.

7 tbsp/100 g butter, plus extra for greasing

12 sage leaves

2 eggs

1½ tbsp/20 g superfine/caster sugar

scant ½ cup/100 g pumpkin purée

½ cup/70 g self-rising/self-raising flour

⅓ cup/50 g ground almonds

salt and black pepper

a 12-hole large madeleine pan, greased with butter

a pastry/piping bag fitted with a large round tip/nozzle

MAKES 12

Set a skillet/frying pan over a gentle heat, add the butter, and heat until foamy. Add the sage leaves and cook for a few minutes until the leaves are slightly crispy, then remove the leaves with a slotted spoon and reserve the butter. Place one sage leaf into each hole of the greased madeleine pan, securing in place in the center with a little butter.

For the madeleine mixture, whisk together the eggs and sugar in a large mixing bowl until the mixture is thick and creamy. Add the pumpkin purée, flour, and almonds and whisk in. Add the cooled, melted sage-infused butter from the skillet and mix together well. Season with salt and pepper, then spoon the batter into the pastry bag and chill in the refrigerator for 1 hour.

Preheat the oven to 350°F (180°C) Gas 4.

Pipe the mixture into the holes of the Madeleine pan, then bake in the preheated oven for about 15–20 minutes until golden brown and the madeleines spring back to your touch. They are best eaten warm and on the day they are made.

WHOLEMEAL SPELT & PUMPKIN SEED MUFFINS

2 eggs

5 tbsp/80 g golden superfine/caster sugar

3 tbsp/50 ml vegetable oil (or groundnut or sunflower)

1 cup plus 2 tbsp/150 g wholemeal spelt flour

1½ tsp baking powder

1 tsp ground cinnamon

1 small carrot, shredded/grated

1 small apple, peeled, cored, and diced

2 tbsp/20 g pumpkin seeds

TOPPING

3 tbsp/30 g pumpkin seeds

light brown soft sugar, to sprinkle

a 6-hole muffin pan, lined with large paper cases

MAKES 6

These spelt muffins are light and nutty with hints of cinnamon and apple.

Preheat the oven to 350°F (180°C) Gas 4.

Put the eggs, sugar, and oil in a mixing bowl and mix well until you have a smooth liquid. Mix the flour, baking powder, and cinnamon together in a separate bowl, then mix into the wet ingredients. Stir in the carrot, apple, and pumpkin seeds until evenly mixed.

Fill each muffin case about two-thirds full with batter. Scatter the pumpkin seeds for the topping over the muffins and finish with a sprinkling of sugar. Bake in the preheated oven for 25 minutes. Do not be tempted to open the oven door halfway through baking as it might cause the muffins to sink. When they are ready, they should be well risen and springy to the touch.

Muffins are always best eaten warm from the oven, but if you have some left over you can refresh them with a quick flash in the microwave. Store in an airtight container for 2–3 days.

PUMPKIN SEED BARS WITH FRUIT & NUTS

7 tbsp/100 g butter

¼ cup/50 g extra virgin coconut oil

¾ cup/150 g granulated/caster sugar

3 tbsp light corn/golden syrup

½ cup/80 g self-rising/self-raising flour

2 eggs, beaten

2 cups/150 g desiccated coconut

1 cup/100 g shelled unsalted pistachios

½ cup/60 g pumpkin seeds

½ cup/60 g sunflower seeds

½ cup/60 g pine nuts

1 cup/150 g raisins or golden raisins/sultanas

a 12 x 8-inch/30 x 20-cm deep-sided baking pan, greased and base-lined

MAKES 14 BARS

These hearty bars, packed with nuts, seeds, and dried fruit, are perfect for a quick energy fix.

Preheat the oven to 350°F (180°C) Gas 4.

Put the butter, coconut oil, sugar, and syrup in a large saucepan and heat until the butter has melted. Take off the heat and leave to cool slightly.

Sift the flour into a mixing bowl and add all the remaining ingredients. Stir with a wooden spoon until everything is well mixed together. Pour in the cooled butter mixture and mix together.

Tip the mixture into the prepared pan and press down using the back of a spoon. Bake in the preheated oven for 20–25 minutes, until the top is golden brown and the mixture feels firm to the touch. Let cool completely in the pan then tip out onto a chopping board and cut into bars to serve.

These bars will keep for up to 5 days if stored in an airtight container.

PUMPKIN SEED COOKIES

Seeds contain lots of nutrients that are an important part of a good diet. A great way to feed them to your family is to hide them in delicious cookies, and these are really quick and easy to make.

1½ cups/200 g self-rising/raising flour

1 stick/125 g butter, diced

⅔ cup/125 g light brown/muscovado sugar

1 egg, beaten

½ cup/75 g pumpkin seeds

non-stick or buttered baking dish

MAKES 20

Preheat the oven to 350°F (180°C) Gas 4.

Put the flour, butter, and sugar in a bowl and mix with a fork until the mixture resembles breadcrumbs. Add the egg and seeds, mix again, and form into a ball.

Lightly flour a work surface and use your hands to roll the dough into a sausage shape about 8 inches/20 cm long. Cut into 20 slices and place on a non-stick or buttered baking sheet. Bake in the preheated oven for about 12–15 minutes.

When done, let cool on a wire rack, then store in an airtight container.

PUMPKIN SPICE & ALL THINGS NICE

Cakes, pies & other sweet treats

CLASSIC PUMPKIN PIE

13 oz./375 g ready-made pie crust dough/sweet pastry

1–2 tbsp milk

1 x 14-oz./425-g can puréed pumpkin pie filling

2 eggs

1 egg yolk

¾ cup/150 g light brown soft sugar

1 tsp ground cinnamon

½ tsp ground ginger

a pinch of grated nutmeg

a pinch of ground cloves

a pinch of salt

½ cup/125 ml heavy/double cream

2–3 tsp granulated/caster sugar

confectioners'/icing sugar, for dusting

a 9-inch/23-cm round pie dish

a small star-shaped cutter

SERVES 6

An American holiday recipe that can be whipped up in no time using shop-bought sweet pastry and pumpkin purée.

Preheat the oven to 350°F (180°C) Gas 4 and place a baking sheet on the middle shelf to preheat.

Sprinkle a little flour on a clean work surface. Roll out the dough to a thickness of about ⅛ inch/ 2–3 mm. Carefully lift up the pastry (it may help to lift it while on the rolling pin) and lay it in the pie dish. Trim any excess pastry from around the edge with a small knife.

Gather up any scraps of dough, knead very lightly to bring together into a ball, and roll out again. Use the star-shaped cutter to stamp out lots of stars. Brush the edges of the pie with a little milk and stick the pastry stars, slightly overlapping, all around the edge. Chill the pastry case in the refrigerator while you prepare the filling.

Put the puréed pumpkin, whole eggs and yolk, brown sugar, cinnamon, ginger, nutmeg, cloves, salt, and cream in a large bowl and whisk until well mixed and smooth. Carefully pour the mixture into the pie dish, brush the stars with a little more milk and scatter the granulated sugar over them. Put the pie on the hot baking sheet in the preheated oven

and bake for about 35 minutes, or until the filling has set and the pastry is golden brown around the edges.

Remove the pie from the oven and let cool to room temperature before dusting with confectioners' sugar.

PUMPKIN PIE POPS

If you want something fun and warming to serve at a Halloween party, look no further than these cute and tasty jack-o-lantern pie pops.

¾ cup/140 g canned pumpkin purée

1 tbsp pumpkin pie spice*

1 extra-large/UK large egg, plus extra for egg wash

¼ tsp salt

⅓ cup/75 ml runny honey

13 oz./375 g ready-made pie crust dough/sweet pastry

a 3-inch/7.5-cm pumpkin-shaped cookie cutter

24 wooden popsicle sticks

MAKES 24

*If you can't buy pumpkin pie spice, make your own by blending 1 tsp ground cinnamon, ½ tsp ground ginger, and ¼ tsp each ground nutmeg and allspice. Any leftover can be stored in an airtight container.

Heat the pumpkin purée and spice in a saucepan set over a medium heat, just long enough for the spices to become fragrant. Remove from the heat and pour into a bowl to cool. When the filling comes to room temperature, whisk in the egg, salt, and honey and chill in the refrigerator.

Put the pastry on a floured work surface and roll out to ⅛-inch/3-mm thick. Stamp out 48 pastry shapes using the cookie cutter. Use a sharp knife to cut out scary or fun faces from 24 of the shapes and put in the refrigerator to chill for about 30 minutes.

Preheat the oven to 350°F (180°C) Gas 4.

Take the pastry pumpkins from the refrigerator, coat with egg wash, and lay on a baking sheet. Put a wooden stick in the middle of the plain shapes, then add 1–2 tablespoons of pumpkin filling. Top each with a pastry shape with a cut-out face and seal the edges of the pies by crimping the pastry with a fork. Brush all the pies with egg wash. Bake in the middle of the preheated oven for about 15–20 minutes, or until golden brown. Take care when serving as the filling may still be hot.

MINI PUMPKIN CHEESECAKES

5 tbsp/75 g butter

4½ oz./125 g shortcake or shortbread cookies, broken into pieces

7 oz./200 g cream cheese

3½ oz./100 g soft curd cheese

3½ oz./100 g canned pumpkin purée

½ cup/100 g superfine/caster sugar

2 eggs, lightly beaten

2 pinches each of ground cloves, ginger, allspice, and nutmeg

orange sanding sugar, to decorate (optional)

NUTMEG FROSTING

¼ cup/50 g superfine/caster sugar

3½ oz./100 g cream cheese

½ tsp freshly grated nutmeg

a 12-hole muffin pan, lined with paper cases

MAKES 12

Have fun with these for Halloween and decorate with sugarcraft sprinkles.

Preheat the oven to 300°F (150°C) Gas 3.

Melt the butter in a pan and leave to cool slightly. Grind the cookies to crumbs in a food processor. Add all but 1 tablespoon of the melted butter (reserve this for the frosting) and whizz to combine. Divide between the cupcake cases and press down firmly with the back of a teaspoon.

Put the cream cheese, curd cheese, pumpkin purée, sugar, beaten eggs, and spices in an electric mixer. Whisk until smooth and combined. Tip the mixture into a pitcher/jug, then pour it into the cupcake cases, dividing it equally.

Bake the cakes in the preheated oven for 15 minutes. Let cool completely—they will set as they cool.

To make the frosting, whisk the ingredients together (including the reserved butter) and put a spoonful on the top of each cheesecake.

Sprinkle with sanding sugar, if you like. They are soft-set, so they are best eaten with teaspoons.

PUMPKIN CUPCAKES

The light sprinkling of ground cinnamon over the cream cheese frosting gives these cupcakes a pretty finish.

1 cup/120 g all-purpose/plain flour

scant ¾ cup/140 g granulated/caster sugar

1 tbsp baking powder

1½ tsp ground cinnamon, plus extra to decorate

a pinch of salt

3 tbsp/40 g unsalted butter, at room temperature

½ cup/120 ml whole milk

2 eggs

6½ oz./200 g canned pumpkin purée

1 quantity Frosting (see page 112), but omit the nutmeg

a 12-hole cupcake pan, lined with paper cases

MAKES 12

Preheat the oven to 325°F (170°C) Gas 3.

Put the flour, sugar, baking powder, cinnamon, salt, and butter in a freestanding electric mixer with a paddle attachment (or use a handheld electric whisk) and beat on slow speed until you get a sandy consistency and everything is combined. Gradually pour in half the milk and beat until well mixed.

Add the eggs to the mix and beat well (scrape any unmixed ingredients from the side of the bowl with a rubber spatula). Stir in the pumpkin purée by hand until evenly dispersed. Use some of the remaining milk if needed to loosen the mixture.

Spoon the mixture into the paper cases until two-thirds full and bake in the preheated oven for about 20 minutes, or until light golden and the sponge bounces back when touched. Leave the cupcakes to cool slightly in the pan before turning out onto a wire cooling rack to cool completely.

When the cupcakes are cold, spoon the frosting on top and finish with a light sprinkling of cinnamon.

PUMPKIN & ALMOND CAKE

This cake tastes even better the day after it's been baked, so cover it loosely with foil and enjoy any leftovers the next day.

1 cup/220 g granulated/caster sugar

2/3 cup/150 g butter, at room temperature

4 eggs, whisked

1⅓ cups/175 g all-purpose/plain flour

1 tbsp ground cinnamon

1 tsp ground cloves

1 tsp vanilla extract

1 x 15-oz./425-g can natural/unsweetened pumpkin purée

1 cup/100 g ground almonds

a 8-inch/20-cm round cake pan, lined with baking parchment

SERVES 8

Preheat the oven to 400°F (200°C) Gas 6.

Cream the sugar and butter together in a bowl, then add the whisked eggs and flour along with the spices and vanilla extract, mixing until smooth. Briefly whisk in the pumpkin purée, then mix in the ground almonds.

Once fully combined, pour the cake mixture into the lined cake pan and bake in the preheated oven for 1 hour. Leave to cool in the pan on a wire rack before serving.

Note: this cake is delicious served with a large spoonful of crème fraîche and a generous sprinkle of ground cinnamon.

SPICED PUMPKIN CHEESECAKE

Scatter toasted pumpkin seeds on top to add a bit of crunchiness or drizzle with caramel sauce for some extra indulgence.

1 lb. 5 oz./600 g gingernut cookies/biscuits

¾–1 stick/75–100 g unsalted butter, melted

½ cup/100 g superfine/caster sugar

½ cup/110 g dark brown soft sugar

1½ tsp ground cinnamon

½ tsp freshly grated nutmeg

1 tbsp ground ginger

1 tsp ground allspice

½ tsp salt

1 tsp vanilla extract

1 lb. 9 oz./700 g cream cheese

3 eggs

3 tbsp whipping cream

2 tbsp Bourbon

1 x 15-oz./425-g can of pumpkin purée

TOPPING

1⅓ cups/300 ml whipping cream

⅔ cup/60 g confectioners'/icing sugar

3 oz./75 g crystallized ginger, chopped

3 tbsp pumpkin seeds, toasted

a 10-inch/25-cm cake pan, greased and base-lined with baking parchment

SERVES 10–12

Preheat the oven to 240°F (125°C) Gas 1.

To make the crust, crush the gingernut cookies until you get fine crumbs. Add the melted butter—the amount of butter you will need is variable. Test by grabbing a bit of the mixture and squeezing into your hand to make a ball, then releasing your hand. The mixture should hold its shape, but also fall apart when touched slightly. If it doesn't hold its shape, add more butter, otherwise the cookie will dissolve into the cheesecake and you'll have no crust. If it holds its shape too well, add more cookies to absorb the butter, otherwise your crust will be too hard.

Press the mixture into the prepared cake pan and pat level.

Put the sugar, all the spices, and the vanilla into a large mixing bowl and stir until well combined. Add the cream cheese and beat until well mixed and the sugar has dissolved.

Slowly incorporate the eggs, one at a time, beating until thoroughly combined before adding the next. Scrape the side of the bowl regularly to make sure everything is incorporated. Stir in the whipping cream and bourbon. Fold in the pumpkin purée until well combined.

Pour the mixture into the cake pan over the crust and bake in the preheated oven for 1 hour until the middle is still slightly jiggly and the top doesn't look shiny or wet any more.

Remove from the oven and let cool in the pan for 1 hour. Refrigerate overnight.

When you are ready to serve, unmold the cheesecake by turning it upside down on a serving plate or board, then turning it upright again.

To make the topping, put the cream and confectioners' sugar in a bowl and, using an electric mixer with whisk attachment (or an electric whisk), whisk to soft peaks. Spread the topping casually over the cheesecake and top with the crystallized ginger and pumpkin seeds.

PUMPKIN & CINNAMON STRUDEL

This crumbly, heavenly phyllo/filo strudel is made with creamy, sweet pumpkin and a hint of cinnamon.

7 oz./200 g pumpkin, peeled

½ tsp ground cinnamon

¼ cup/50 g golden superfine/caster sugar

3 large sheets of thick phyllo/filo pastry (18½ x 12½ inches/47 x 32 cm)*

1 tbsp vegetable oil

confectioners'/icing sugar, to dust

a baking sheet, greased

MAKES 6 SLICES

* If you can't find large sheets of phyllo/filo pastry, just use smaller sheets and overlap them to make the correct size.

Preheat the oven to 325°F (170°C) Gas 3.

Grate the pumpkin and squeeze out any excess water. Put in a bowl and mix with the cinnamon and sugar.

Take one sheet of phyllo pastry, lay it on the prepared baking sheet and lightly brush with oil. Place a second sheet of pastry on top and lightly brush with oil. Repeat with the third sheet of pastry.

Spoon the pumpkin filling along one longer side of the phyllo sheets, leaving a ¾-inch/2-cm gap on either side and spreading the filling about 2 inches/5 cm wide. Fold the longer side of the pastry, nearest the filling, in about ¾ inch/2 cm, then roll the pastry up, tucking in the sides as you go.

Brush the top of the strudel with a little more oil and bake in the preheated oven for 25 minutes. The strudel should be pale gold. Remove from the oven and leave to cool for 5 minutes. Dust liberally with confectioners' sugar and serve warm.

SWEET PUMPKIN, PECAN & MAPLE SYRUP TART

Pumpkin cuts through the rich toffee of a traditional pecan pie, making it softer and more tender, while the maple syrup adds a smokiness.

13 oz./375 g ready-made pie crust dough/sweet pastry

2 tbsp/25 g unsalted butter

2½ cups/300 g pumpkin or squash, peeled, seeded, and shredded/grated

¼ cup/50 g light muscovado sugar

2 tbsp bourbon or rum

⅔ cup/100 g pecan halves, half chopped

2 eggs

grated zest of 1 unwaxed lemon

⅔ cup/150 ml dark maple syrup

½ tsp vanilla extract

⅔ cup/150 ml heavy/double cream

confectioners'/icing sugar, to dust

a deep, 9-inch/22–23-cm loose-bottomed metal tart pan

SERVES 8

Roll the dough out on a floured work surface and line the tart pan. Chill for 30 minutes.

Preheat the oven to 375°F (190°C) Gas 5.

Support the sides of the tart with foil and bake in the preheated oven for 12 minutes. Remove the foil, press down any air bubbles in the base and bake for another 10 minutes or until pale brown. Remove from the oven and reduce the heat to 350°F (180°C) Gas 4.

Meanwhile, melt the butter in a skillet/frying pan and gently fry the pumpkin for about 5 minutes until tender and lightly browned. Increase the heat a little, add 2 tablespoons of the muscovado sugar and

cook until the sugar caramelizes and melts around the pumpkin.

Add the bourbon and cook briskly until a sticky syrup forms, then mix in the chopped pecans. Spoon the pumpkin mixture into the tart case and arrange the pecan halves on top.

Beat together the eggs, remaining sugar, lemon zest, maple syrup, and vanilla extract, then gradually beat in the cream. Pour the mixture into the tart case. Bake in the still-hot oven for 35–40 minutes, until puffed up and the center retains a very slight wobble.

PUMPKIN LATTE

Perfect for any wintertime party, this thick, richly spiced latte is flavored with sweetened pumpkin. If you can find canned sweetened pumpkin purée, then use this and omit the sugar in the recipe.

1½ cups/375 ml milk of your choice

3½ oz./100 g cooked sweet pumpkin, mashed (or canned pumpkin purée)

3 tbsp brown sugar (omit if using canned purée)

¼ tsp ground sweet cinnamon

1 cup/250 ml freshly brewed French press/cafetière or filter coffee

whipped cream (canned is fine) and cinnamon sugar, to serve

balloon whisk

SERVES 4

Put the milk, pumpkin, sugar (if using), and cinnamon in a saucepan and heat gently, whisking constantly until the mixture just reaches boiling point. Transfer to four cups or heatproof glasses and stir in the coffee.

Top with whipped cream and a dusting of cinnamon sugar. Serve at once.

INDEX

RECIPE CREDITS

Nadia Arumugam
Beef Stew with Pumpkin & Szechuan pepper

Ghillie Başan
Roasted Pumpkin Wedges with Lime Zest & Spices

Fiona Beckett
Roast Pumpkin & Garlic Polenta

Maxine Clark
Pumpkin & Pea Risotto with Toasted Pumpkin Seeds

Megan Davies
Pumpkin & Chicory Pasta Bake

Ross Dobson
Pumpkin & Gorgonzola Risotto
Spiced Pumpkin & Spelt Salad
Tagliatelle with Pan-Fried Pumpkin & Red Pepper Oil

Acland Geddes & Pedro Da Silva
Pearl Barley & Pumpkin Salad
Roast Pumpkin with Sweet Potato Mash & Marshmallows

Brian Glover
Mini Cheese Fondues
Pan-fried Pumpkin & Walnut Pasta with Parsley & Walnut Sauce
Pumpkin & Goat Cheese Tarts
Pumpkin Gnocchi with Buttery Sage Breadcrumbs
Roasted Flat Mushrooms with Spiced Pumpkin & Chickpea Stuffing
Roasted Pumpkin, Chicken, & Lentil Salad with Preserved Lemon Dressing
Spiced Pumpkin & Feta Pastries

Spicy Pumpkin & Coconut Soup
Sweet Pumpkin, Pecan, & Maple Syrup Tart

Dunja Gulin
Adzuki Bean & Pumpkin Stew
Pumpkin, carrot, & red lentil soup

Tori Haschka
Roast Apple & Pumpkin Soup with Maple Nut Crumble

Carol Hilker
Pumpkin Pie Pops

Kathy Kordalis
Pumpkin, Blue Cheese, & Sage Pizza

Tarek Malouf (& the Hummingbird Bakers)
Pumpkin Cupcakes

Theo A, Michaels
Pumpkin & Almond Cake

Hannah Miles
Pumpkin & Goat Cheese Pancakes
Pumpkin Latte
Pumpkin Loaves
Pumpkin Madeleines with Sage
Pumpkin Scones
Pumpkin Seed Bars with Fruit and Nuts
Roasted Pumpkin Soup

Elsa Peterson Schepelern
Pumpkin Raisin Bread
Stuffed Sugar Pumpkins with Pesto & Goat Cheese

Isadora Popovic
Pumpkin & Cinnamon Strudel
Wholemeal Carrot, Apple, & Pumpkin Muffins

Sarah Randall
Mini Pumpkin Cheesecakes

Annie Rigg
Classic Pumpkin Pie

Laura Santini
Pumpkin & Sage Pasta

Fiona Smith
Prosciutto & Pumpkin Terrine

Leah Vanderveldt
Pumpkin & Black Bean Chilli
Thai Pumpkin & Vegetable Curry

Bea Vo
Spiced Pumpkin Cheesecake

Fran Warde
Pumpkin Seed Cookies

Laura Washburn Hutton
Pumpkin, Corn, & Bread Pudding with Cheese & Chives
Pumpkin & Rice Gratin
Pumpkin & Sage Mac 'n' Cheese
Roasted Pumpkin Grilled Cheese Sandwich with Sage Butter
Roasted Pumpkin with Spiced Lentils, Goat Cheese, & Walnuts

Lindy Wildsmith
Pumpkin & Tomato Chutney

Belinda Williams
Pumpkin & Mushroom Soup

PHOTOGRAPHY CREDITS

Caroline Arber
Page 105.

Martin Brigdale
Pages 57, 66, 86.

Peter Cassidy
Pages 1, 3, 9, 10, 20, 32, 36, 43, 45, 46, 48, 50, 55, 65, 70, 81, 89, 90, 100, 106, 114, 120, 123.

Tara Fisher
Page 69.

Richard Jung
Pages 24, 30, 58, 75, 82.

Mowie Kay
Pages 40, 117.

Lisa Linder
Page 109.

Jason Lowe
Page 85.

Alex Luck
Page 16.

Steve Painter
Pages 2, 12, 35, 39, 72, 110.

Rita Platts
Page 76.

William Reavell
Pages 8, 19, 22, 95, 96, 99, 102.

Christopher Scholey
Page 79.

Debi Treloar
Pages 61, 92.

Isobel Weld
Page 15.

Kate Whittaker
Pages 5, 53, 62, 113, 119.

Clare Winfield
Pages 27, 46, 124.